INSIDE MY HEART

GUIDED JOURNAL

INSIDE MY HEART

Choosing to Live with Passion and Purpose

GUIDED JOURNAL

ROBIN MCGRAW

THOMAS NELSON
Since 1798

NASHVILLE   DALLAS   MEXICO CITY   RIO DE JANEIRO   BEIJING

Published in Nashville, Tennessee, by Thomas Nelson, Inc.

Nelson Books titles may be purchased in bulk for educational, business, fund-raising, or sales promotional use. For information, please e-mail SpecialMarkets@ThomasNelson.com.

ISBN: 1-4185-1436-5
ISBN-13: 978-1-4185-1436-5

Printed in the United States of America
07 08 09 10 — 5 4 3 2 1

This book is dedicated to the millions of women who have so selflessly nurtured and cared for others as a wife, mother, daughter, sister and friend. My heart is to help women realize that they should never settle for anything less than the best for themselves and in their relationships.

CONTENTS

Chapter One

FROM MY HEART TO YOURS

I am on a mission to get you excited about your life.

And let me tell you, I'm excited—not only excited to be a woman, but to be a wife, a mother, an enthusiastic homemaker, and now an author. My greatest hope is that what I put down in these pages may inspire and help you and other women by offering an honest look inside at who I am: how I've lived my life, the struggles I've faced, the decisions I've made, and how and why I've made them. The journey hasn't always been easy and it sure hasn't always been fun, and I've had my share of disappointments along the way. But it has all made me who I am today.

Stop and take a moment now just for you. Push everything else aside and embrace this time to reflect on the life you've lived thus far, and on the life you are living now. This is what this guided journal is all about—to make a choice to put yourself first and to make the time to think about and create the life you want. Maybe it's not the life you have now, but do you know that it can be? That the life you dream of is one you deserve to live?

So take a few (or many) moments to think about your life—the easy times and the hard times; the joys and the disappointments; the struggles and the triumphs. Then record those significant times in the following space.

I'm smart enough now to value the experiences I've had over the half-century I've been in this world, and I know that the ones that count are all a result of the choices I've made. But I also know that many people aren't aware that there are choices to be made, that they do have control over a lot of what happens to them. The freedom to choose the way we live our lives is one of the great gifts we've been given.

That is worth saying again: The freedom to choose the way we live our lives is one of the great gifts we've been given.

How do you feel about that statement? Do you believe it is true?

Have you been living your life with this perspective of freedom of choice? If so, describe how this freedom is allowing you to live. If what I have just said is news to you, how could this perspective change your life?

A lot of people go through life without really thinking about who they are or why they do the things they do. It's as if we're living on autopilot, staring straight ahead without seeing anything other than what's right in front of our faces. I know what this feels like because it's happened to me.

I'm usually able to snap out of my daze and get back in control pretty quickly, but I know how easy it is to go passive. We do things or agree to things or accept whatever comes our way without considering whether or not it's right for us. And by passively accepting whatever happens, we give up chances every day to create the lives we want.

It *doesn't* have to be that way.

You can make choices in your life—in fact, you must make choices—in order to have the life you want. And whether or not you're aware of it, you do make choices all the time; even choosing not to choose is a choice.

Do you ever feel that you are living your life on autopilot? What do you think causes you to live in a daze?

To what degree do you feel actively in control of what's happening in your life?

Are you naturally a proactive decision-maker, or do you tend to be more passive?

Out of the many, many choices you've made in your life, consider three significant ones you've made.

Specifically, how has each choice benefited you, and how has each one challenged you?

Think of a time when you have chosen not to choose. What was the result? Do you recognize any area(s) of your life in which you consistently avoid making choices, and just let things happen as they will?

Are you content to continue with your current track of decision-making?

I live every day of my life as an adventure, and I approach every aspect of my life as an event. Life has tried to knock that spirit out of me, and you probably know what that feels like. But I always have faith that things will get better. And it doesn't matter how old I get; I still wake up every morning grateful to be alive and healthy, and passionate about making the most of the day. And while I've always known this about myself, it wasn't until I sat down to write this book that I thought about how I got that way, and how it is that my life turned out the way it has. I simply cannot imagine wanting to be anything or anyone other than who I am: a freethinking woman, wife of the man I love, and mother of two grown sons.

What events or people in your life have threatened to knock the spirit out of you? What happened? Did they succeed? Did you recover? How did you handle it?

Whether you know it or not, you're constantly writing the "book" of your own life (regardless of whether you actually ever write anything down or not). You are ever-evolving, ever-changing, ever-growing. Keep this in mind as you go through this journal. Some things in your past will be hard to remember, while you will delight in remembering others. Embrace every step in your journey, for they have made you the woman you are.

~

I believe I'm smarter today than I was yesterday, and I know I'm a whole lot smarter than I was ten, twenty, or thirty years ago. I don't know if fifty is the new thirty, but I do know that I'm in my fifties now and I love it. I also know that I didn't become who I am through dumb luck; I did it by listening to God's voice, knowing myself, and using all of that knowledge to create the life I wanted.

You see, I absolutely believe that in order for a woman to experience happiness, fulfillment, and peace, she needs to know two things: who she is, and who she is meant to be. They're not quite the same thing: the first one has to do with the reality of your life, and the second one has to do with your purpose for being in this world, which is something each of us has to discover for herself and cannot be dictated by any other person in our lives— not by our husbands, parents, children, employers, or friends.

I think it's getting harder and harder to tell the difference between who we are and who we're meant to be. So much of the time, we lose ourselves just trying to keep up with the frantic pace of life. We drag ourselves out of bed in the morning, already half an hour behind, and spend much of the day responding to the needs and demands of others. Somewhere along the line, we often lose track of the essential feminine self—that unique, life-giving entity that invigorates our beings and warms the souls of the people we love.

> I absolutely believe that in order for a woman to experience happiness, fulfillment, and peace, she needs to know two things: who she is, and who she is meant to be.

But we don't have to lose that feminine self, and the way to hold on to her is to accept nothing less than being simply the best—the best we can be in the roles we choose for ourselves: wife, mother, daughter, sister, and friend. I believe we were put on this earth to enjoy lives of joy and abundance, and that is what I want for you and for me. I want to get you excited about whatever phase of life you're in, excited about being a woman in this day and time, excited about being the woman that God created you to be.

I sincerely believe that God has created each of us—that means you!— uniquely and with great intention. You were created with specific gifts and talents—all of which are a big part of who you are.

Do you know that you are special and that you have something to offer the world that no one else has? What do you think is the difference in knowing who you are and who you were meant to be?

Do you feel that your life is one of joy and abundance? Why or why not?

Are you excited about your life? If so, what excites you? If not, what do you think is holding you back from feeling that excitement?

I believe that in this life, we are defined not by the station in life into which we are born, nor by our pedigree, race, or religion, but by the choices we make. By choosing to live with passion and purpose, I have fashioned a rich and rewarding life—not because I'm special, or a genius, or born under a lucky star. Far from it.

My goal for this book is to tell everyone who reads it about the power of choosing her life rather than taking it as it comes along—not so you'll make the same choices I made, but so you can make the choices that are right for you. I'm not a professional expert and I'm certainly not an expert on

> I believe that in this life, we are defined not by the station in life into which we are born, nor by our pedigree, race, or religion, but by the choices we make.

your life, but I am an expert on mine, and that is what I hope to share with you.

It's not my intention to give people advice on how to solve their problems (I leave that to my husband). But I've had my share of struggles over the years, and I know a thing or two about what has worked for me in this life. I have learned which battles to pick, when and how to push back, and how to bend without breaking. In short, I have figured out how not to lose "me" in the course of being so many things to so many people in so many areas of my life. I have chosen to be an active participant in my life rather than a spectator, and in so doing I have chosen how to be a woman, how to be a wife, and how to be a mother in ways that are uniquely my own. I offer the stories of these choices as evidence of the power of sheer determination, will, and faith in God.

> My goal for this book is to tell everyone who reads it about the power of choosing her life rather than taking it as it comes along—not so you'll make the same choices I made, but so you can make the choices that are right for you.

Do you believe you can change your life with the choices you make? Why or why not?

In what specific ways have you chosen how to be a woman, a wife, a mother, a friend in ways that are uniquely your own?

To be sure, I'm not doing it alone. I wake up every morning and I thank God for everything that is good, right, and true in my life. I am thankful for all the people in my life whose love and care are sources of constant rejuvenation for my spirit. I am thankful for the gift of free will and for the chance to choose the life God means for me to lead.

Not least, I am thankful for the opportunity to reach out to women everywhere, and touch their lives by telling them about mine. I want to reach out to all women—older and younger, married and single, women who are mothers and those who are not, women who work outside the home and those who don't.

As I write this book, I find myself looking deeply into the reservoir of memory and seeing reflections of things I haven't thought about in years, sometimes decades. When I reach out to touch them, I do so gently. God has blessed me so that I can still feel the touch of my mother's hand and see my father's smile. This is what I offer, with equal parts humility, wonder, and truth. Should any of it touch you in any way, I shall consider myself abundantly blessed.

Before we move on, let me ask: What do you hope to gain from your time spent on this journal?

A Woman's Heart (and Mind)

"Being a woman is hard work."
—Maya Angelou

As women, we see the world in unique and wonderful ways. Some of us are very nurturing; others are very organized. Some are incredible hostesses; others of us love nothing better than a good meal out. But we can all count on having one thing in common—a love for shoes. If you could see my closet, you'd understand: I must have a hundred pairs of shoes, and I can still find room for more. And girls, I know you know what I mean. A woman can never have too many shoes.

This is something that most men just don't understand. Phillip thinks three pairs of shoes is one pair too many. And his opinion of chocolate is that it's just another snack—like beer nuts, or a piece of fruit. I've got a huge bowl of fruit sitting on my kitchen counter, and I like a crisp apple or a juicy orange as much as the next girl. But to think of a melt-in-your-mouth bittersweet truffle as no different than a beer nut? I just don't get it.

It is amazing how vastly different men can be from us. Often, it seems that they have their own language and view of the world in general. When it comes to Phillip's work, he's the most thorough guy in the world. But when it comes to personal matters, he never asks the right questions. He'll come home after work and say, "Oh, guess what? Joe and Elizabeth had their baby today." I'll get all excited and start asking questions.

"Oh my gosh, what'd they have?"

"I don't know," he'll say.

"You didn't ask?"

"No."

"Well, okay," I'll say, pressing on. "What did they name it?'"

"I don't know."

"Well then, how's Elizabeth doing?"

"I'm sure she's exhausted, Robin. She just had a baby."

Now, you ask a woman about some couple's blessed event, and she'll tell you the baby's name, how much it weighed, how long it was, how long the labor was, how many pushes it took to squeeze it out, and whether or not they're planning on having another one—and that's just for starters. But when it comes to women and what's important to them, men just don't ask the right questions.

What have you found to be the biggest differences between men and women?

What do you feel are your strongest and most positive qualities as a woman?

One time when we were newlyweds living in a little apartment outside of Dallas, way before Phillip was Dr. Phil but when he was already a psychologist, I asked one too many questions. I was working during the day and going to college at night, and Phillip was working on his doctorate at the University of North Texas. We were both at home studying, and Phillip was working to perfect the skill of performing psychological assessments on patients. I said, "Do you want to practice on me?" (In retrospect, that qualified me as an idiot. He might have discovered my shoe obsession and headed for the hills!)

He said he was going to ask me a lot of questions that I had to answer as honestly as I could, and I figured, how hard can it be? I'm married to the man, after all; he knows everything about me. So he started doing the profile and I started squirming. He asked me all these questions about my mother and my father, and how I felt about my brother and my sisters, and he wrote everything down. The more questions he asked, the more I found myself stammering and stalling for time, and I was getting so nervous I finally got up on my tiptoes and looked him right in the eye and said, "Now, listen buddy—this assessment is over." It was dawning on me what all this man was learning. I said, "Okay, I know I said I'd do this with you, but don't you be using this test on me, and don't you be analyzing me when I don't know it. If you're going to analyze me, it'll be when I ask you to." I set that rule down way back then.

I never again asked Phillip to analyze me or my behaviors the way he would do for a patient. I guess it's similar to the way surgeons aren't supposed to operate on family members because they might be too emotionally involved to use their best medical judgment. And while doing brain surgery on your wife is a lot different than trying to get inside her head with a psychological profile, the whole thing was still a little too close for my comfort level.

Are you an "open book" to anyone you may meet, or do you require a certain level of trust and comfort with someone before you can open up to them?

How do you feel when someone gets a little too personal with you? Why do you think you react that way?

Having trusted confidants—people who make us feel safe, secure, and free to open up and share our hearts—is so important. As women, we truly need those people in our lives to feel we are understood and known.

Do you have a trusted confidant in your life? Who is it and how does that person make you feel?

My nurturing nature became highly developed early on in my life. I think a lot of that has to do with the fact that I have a twin brother. I loved telling him, "Don't worry, I'll always be there for you and I'll always take care of you," when we were really young.

I think that's when my real love of mothering started, because I always wanted to take care of Roger, whether he wanted me to or not. We moved around a lot when I was a kid, and we were always transferring to different schools. I remember being in first grade and starting at a new school, and the teacher wanted Roger and me to stay late one day so she could test our reading skills and know where to place us in reading class.

She sat down with Roger at the desk in front of me and told him he would be reading first. So Roger starts reading aloud, "See Spot run." But before he could get to the third word, I was saying it for him. He'd say "See Spot—," and I'd say "run." He'd say, "Jane goes outside—," and I'd chime in, "to play."

After about ten minutes, the teacher said, "Robin honey, you're going to have to let him read his own words." And I was thinking, "Uh-oh, this is not good; she's not going to let me help him." Not that he needed my help, mind you; Roger could read just as well as I could. I just felt an irresistible urge to protect him.

The teacher could see that I was like a little mother hen with him, so the next day she seated him in the first chair of the first row and put me in the last chair of the last row so I couldn't help him. And—I'll never forget this—she said, "All right, children, we're going to learn to spell our names and write them down on the top of the paper." And I'm thinking, *Jameson . . . can Roger spell "Jameson"?* So I stared at Roger and he turned around and looked at me and I whispered "J," hissing it up the row so he could hear me. He turned around and wrote it down and spun around again and I hissed "A," and it went on like that until I had spelled out our last name for him. And I thought, *Okay, this will work out fine.*

Or so I thought until the phone rang that night. It was my teacher, and my mother got on and after a while I heard her saying, "Separate them? Oh, I don't know, that's not going to be good. . . . You can't separate them, they have to be together." It was clear to me as I stood there eavesdropping that the teacher was saying I was helping Roger too much and had to be put in a different class. My mother listened for a while and then said, "All right, but if you do separate them, you're going to have to put him in a room where she can look in and see him and make sure he's okay."

That was my mother for you, doing the right thing for our education but also making sure our needs were considered. And sure enough, the next day they moved Roger to the classroom across the hall, and moved my seat up from the back row to a spot right in front of the doorway where I could look up every few minutes and see that he was okay. I looked across that hall every ten minutes and waited until he looked at me so I could tell from his face that he was okay.

I believe I was put on this earth to be not only a wife and a mother, but to be Phillip's wife and Jay and Jordan's mother, and I really just want to be able to look back on my family—my life's work—and know that I did a good job. I have always felt that motherhood was my calling, and I have always known I am going to do everything I can for my children because I want to be able to say that I'm doing a good job, with no regrets.

> I have always felt that motherhood was my calling, and I have always known I am going to do everything I can for my children because I want to be able to say that I'm doing a good job, with no regrets.

Both Jay and Jordan managed to survive my many mothering mishaps, which is a relief to me. I firmly believe that how happy my sons are is a reflection of who I am and how well I did my job. Being a mother is more than a phase in my life; for me, it's a never-ending mission, my calling here on earth. And when the time comes and I'm standing before my heavenly Father, I just want Him to say to me, "Job well done."

Do you struggle with this question: What is your life's calling? When you're asked this question, do you feel discouraged, that maybe you don't have a calling in life? Even though I have always known my calling was to be a mother, I realize that many women may not know what they truly want in life. And that's OK. But now is the time to begin to discover it!

Right now, take a few minutes to think about what is most important to you in your life. List them in the space provided.

Now consider the list you made above. Could any of the things on your list be your calling? At the end of your life, for what would you most like to be told, "Job well done"?

How are you fulfilling your calling? Or, if your calling is not a present reality for you, why do you feel you're not living that calling and how do you plan to live your calling in the future?

I believe that it is essential to know your life's calling and to live well in that calling. Maybe you need to give yourself a little time to begin to explore this. Take that class you've always wanted to take. Volunteer with an organization that you find interesting. Expand your perspective and plunge into new and different experiences. All of these things will help you begin to discover your life's calling. There are countless good resources and books out there that can help you identify your natural giftedness and learn how to develop and expand it. It may not be an easy process, but it will be worth it!

I want to be proud of myself because I raised decent children. I do not ever want to live with the regret of knowing I could have tried a little harder to help my kids become happy, healthy adults. That doesn't mean I couldn't have done things better or differently. As a young bride and mother, I made all the predictable, typical mistakes and then some. As much as I don't want to admit it (we never do, do we?), there are a few things I wish I'd done differently.

And even though I still cringe when I think about my early attempts to take care of my baby, at the time I really was doing my best. It's always been important for me to know I was doing the best I could at the time I was doing it, even if my best sometimes wasn't all that good. We've all made mistakes in our lives. Big or small, we've all done things we wish we hadn't. And even though we might squirm and feel ashamed when we think about those incidents, we must own up to these mistakes in order to keep moving forward in our lives.

How have you made mistakes in your life? List a few of your mistakes. They can be big, small, seemingly insignificant, or life-changing. We can learn from them all. Be brave; be honest.

A more important question is, what do you do when you make a mistake? Do you try and cover it up, hoping no one else noticed? Do you laugh it off and chalk it up to a lesson learned? Or do you beat yourself up over it, still churning over the incident days or weeks later? How do you handle it?

When you make a mistake—notice I said *when*, not *if*—it's important to remember to give yourself a little grace. As I said, I believe it is important for me to think back on my mistakes and know that I did the best I could at the time, even if it wasn't the best thing for the situation. Can you be kind to yourself and allow yourself the grace to let go of your past mistakes? Is that hard for you to do?

Above, you wrote about a few mistakes that you've made in the past. Think back to one or two of those mistakes. Consider where you were mentally, physically, emotionally, and spiritually at the time of that mistake.

Journal in the space provided about how you did the best you could at the time you were doing it, even if you feel that your best wasn't all that good.

Can you now see that you did the best you could in that situation? What can you learn from that mistake?

When my boys were about to leave for college, I had a choice and I thought, *This is their time and I want them excited about it. If I sit around and cry and say, "Oh, I'm going to miss you, I don't want you to go,"* that would mean I was making their leaving all about me, and it's not about me; it's about them. I would have felt very selfish if I'd expressed my love by telling them, "Once you leave, I am going to get up every day and cry." What a burden to put on them! They've earned the right to go on and live this new phase in life.

And that's why, if I cried about them leaving, it was always in bed at night or in the bathtub (I give myself permission to cry day or night in the bathtub, because it's one my favorite places to be). My tears were for the joy of being their mother. And of course that came to an end, that daily mothering, when they left for college. But what did not come to an end was the joy I felt—and continue to feel—of being their mother.

I've always believed that women and men are fundamentally different, that being a feminine woman is just as powerful as being a manly man; and that's something I wish every woman would think about. If your husband makes fun of your feminine ways, tell him to try living without them for a while.

It's always been important for the men in my life to see and respect every side of me, to see my femininity and my strength, and to see that my femininity *is* my strength.

When you think of femininity, what comes to mind?

Did you include "strength" as one of the characteristics of femininity? Mahatma Gandhi said, "Strength does not come from physical capacity. It comes from an indomitable will." How do you think this quote relates to femininity?

How do you express yourself as a woman? Do you allow yourself to cry, to get emotional, to be protective, to be creative? When and where do you allow yourself to express these things?

How do you feel about being a feminine woman? Have you ever felt that you had to deny your femininity to get ahead in some way? If so, how did that make you feel?

When a man and woman are together, the man needs to feel that he's the stronger one in the room, and I don't have a problem with that. Men were put on this earth to stand in the doorway and protect their women and children, and I say, God bless them. I always make sure Phillip knows that I rely on his strength, and that I would miss him terribly if he weren't there. Which doesn't mean I'm not plenty strong in my own right: I am. It's just that I don't feel a need to compete with him for dominance in our relationship.

So I've always seen the vulnerable side of men: They are very open, they want to be happy, they want to be loved, and they want to get along. They can also be tender and unexpectedly defenseless, and sometimes need to turn to their women for strength. If you give a man a safe haven to show his soft and gentle side, and let him know you still think he's strong, I think it makes for a perfect relationship.

You've got to get beneath the surface to know who a man really is. And what makes men happy is to be accepted. That is why I have chosen to bring a spirit of acceptance to my relationship with Phillip, and to embrace the differences between us rather than resist them. And that is why I don't think we should judge our husbands or the other men in our lives too harshly. We have to accept their ways because that's what makes life interesting. That's another choice I made: to love and accept Phillip as he was, and is, and will be. And boy, have I been tested on that one! After thirty years of marriage, I've had many, many opportunities to learn and grow in the acceptance department. And I've made remarkable progress, considering that I've not always had that accepting spirit.

> That is why I have chosen to bring a spirit of acceptance to my relationship with Phillip, and to embrace the differences between us rather than resist them.

Acceptance of differences, as well as acceptance of each person's hopes, dreams, and aspirations, is a very important part of any relationship.

Is there a relationship in your life in which you have resisted being accepting of your differences with that person? How might your relationship change if you allowed that person to be who they are instead of who you'd like for them to be?

I'll be coming back to this acceptance idea often, because it's such an important part of what makes our marriage work. I know now that just because Phillip loves me doesn't mean he's supposed to think the way I do, or act the way I do, or know you're not supposed to put a thirty-five-dollar bath towel on the garage floor (or your wife in the trunk of your car). I know now that a big part of marriage is not wishing my husband were more like me, but accepting and actually enjoying the fact that he isn't. Relationships, and our lives in general, will never be 100% exactly, positively the way we want them be. And the sooner you can let go of your own expectations and just let others be—really be—who they are, the sooner you will find contentment and joy in those relationships.

Have you been trying to push someone in your life into being something they just are not? How is that affecting your relationship with that person?

What are some ways that you can actively choose to put aside your expectations and let that person be who they are? If you can do this, how could it change your relationship?

It's hard to overestimate the value of acceptance—acceptance of those in your life who you love and, more importantly, acceptance of yourself as the beautiful, strong, independent, and capable woman that you are.

Chapter Three

A DAUGHTER'S HEART:

Choosing My Own Legacy

What comes to mind when you hear someone talk about a *legacy?* Do you think about how your great-great-grandparents immigrated to America from a far-off land? About the amount of money you'll leave to your children one day? About family traditions that are passed down through generations?

I think it's interesting that the dictionary defines *legacy* in two ways. First, as "a gift by will, especially of money or other personal property." Hmm, sounds pretty good, right? Visions of mansions, trust funds, and designer wardrobes come to mind. Unfortunately, most of us won't be inheriting a family fortune any time soon, so the second definition seems more applicable: "something transmitted by or received from an ancestor or predecessor or from the past." That's more of a definition I can relate to. Because whether we like it or not, we are all tied to the past. To those who came before us. We study old, moldy family pictures and search their features for a nose, a smile, an expression that we recognize and identify as like our own. We keep our grandmother's hand-stitched quilt tucked safely away from kids and dogs so that we will have something to remember her by.

Why do we do these things? Because it's important to know where you've come from—and more important, to know *who* you've come from. We look to the past to give us instruction and wisdom for the future. To discover whether or not there are any traditions, family recipes, or practices that we can incorporate into our lives.

Have you ever researched your family legacy, as in creating a family tree or by listening to stories about your great-grandmother's life? What is something you've learned about your family, or a particular family member, that you find intriguing or exciting?

How would you describe your family legacy?

When you think back to your childhood, and to your relationships with your immediate family, what images do you see in your mind? How do you feel? What are the first thoughts, impressions, and memories that pop up without you even having to think about them?

When I think on my childhood, many of my memories center on my family's love. I grew up in Oklahoma with three older sisters, a twin brother, and parents who loved us with all their hearts. They were also crazy about each other, which went a long way toward teaching us kids how a man and woman could live together in a small house, raise five children, and still get along. We never had enough money to buy everything we wanted or needed, yet we always thought of ourselves as loved rather than deprived.

My mother was the sweetest, gentlest woman you could ever meet. She was about five foot four with beautiful blue eyes and very dark hair that she wore short and stylish. She had the most beautiful legs and was kind of plump (after five kids, who can blame her?), but on her it looked good. She was a womanly woman, and she smiled all the time.

I remember her always saying that it was a privilege to be our mother. That was her spirit: She loved being a mother, and I know I get that from her. Georgia Mae Drake Jameson always put her family first, and she did her best to provide us with clean clothes, three meals a day, and all the love we could stand.

She made all my clothes—that is, the ones that weren't handed down from my sisters. My mother was an amazing seamstress. Sewing was a creative outlet for her. She loved going to fabric stores, and she'd come home with armloads of remnants and patterns and trim and lay it all out so she could see what she had to work with. She seldom bought the fabric she wanted because it was too expensive so instead she bought what was left over and stockpiled it. She had towers of fabric stacked up against her bedroom wall because she was planning to make something with it one day.

I've brought a lot of my mother with me. She talked all the time (so do I), and she laughed at everything. We lived paycheck to paycheck, but she had the attitude that when her children were around, it was Christmas every day. She read cookbooks as if they were novels and on Sundays she read the food section in the newspaper. She was always trying new recipes; I'm talking home-style cooking from scratch that made the house smell of warmth and well-being and love. Meatloaf. Fried chicken. Stews. She also loved to make desserts and was a terrific pastry chef. No matter how low on money we were, we always had a new dessert for a treat. It was one of the many ways she showed us that she loved us.

To put it simply, my mother lived for her children. She always put herself last. If there wasn't quite enough food for dinner, she was the one who didn't get a full plate. She'd often be up well past midnight, scrubbing the bathroom floor or ironing my father's shirts or sitting hunched over her sewing machine, making me a skirt or a blouse out of remnants she'd gotten on sale. But even her best efforts could not tame the chaos of being married to an alcoholic. It's not an easy job to love a drinker, but her heart was in her work and she kept us safe and fed and warm whether my dad was around or not. She protected us, and she did her best to preserve the illusion that our household was just like any other, and that everything was fine.

How would you describe your mother?

What are the things that you most love about your mother?

When you close your eyes and think of your mother, what is one vivid memory that comes to mind?

In what ways are you like your mother?

In what ways are you different from your mother?

What are some things you learned from your mother that you have embraced?

What are some things you learned from your mother that you have chosen to leave behind?

As a child of an alcoholic, I grew up surrounded by uncertainty. Ironically, the source of much of that uncertainty was also the person whose ferocious love played a huge part in defining both who I was and who I am, and that person was my father, Jim Jameson. My father absolutely adored me, and I adored him. He was the most loving, giving, protective person, the best man in the world. He was crazy about my mother, and he loved all five of us kids and made each of us feel as if we might just be his favorite. So I woke up every day feeling very, very loved.

For all his flaws, my father was a hard worker. He managed a car dealership Monday through Friday, and moved from lot to lot as I was growing up. My father also bought a small driving range, where people could hit golf balls, as a side business. Someone ran it for him during the week, and my dad would work there on weekends. We were often with him; my sisters, Roger, and I worked there during the summer and after school. We would have to go every Saturday and Sunday to pick up golf balls—thousands of golf balls.

Of course, the reason we couldn't afford help at the driving range was because my father squandered the bulk of his earnings on drinking and gambling, and there wasn't much left for the family. But this lack of money was never discussed; we all just pitched in because this was just the way life was. We didn't feel deprived or needy because my father didn't tell us he had lost two weeks' earnings on his last binge, and my mother didn't mention it either. They just told us we had to help out at the driving range that weekend, and we went.

What strikes me about my childhood is the sense of feeling both very much loved and very uncertain at the same time. I woke up every morning thinking, did Daddy come home last night? And, if he hadn't, is this the day he'll come home? Or if he had been around consistently for a while, I'd wonder, is this the day this man I love so much will start drinking and gambling again? How long will this binge last? Will there be enough money to buy food? Will the electric company cut off the lights again this month? How long will it be before he's back at work during the day and comes home at night and acts like my dad again?

I knew he was a good and wonderful man and I loved him with all my heart. I also knew he had an illness that cheated my sisters, my brother, and me out of the father we yearned for. When I was just a little girl, I wanted more than anything to make my father well. But because I couldn't do that, I decided that I would dedicate my life to undoing the legacy of doubt, pain, fear, and uncertainty that accompanied his great love for us. I forgave him even then, when I was little, but the fear never left. But what makes my story different from some I've heard is that as much as my father's drinking hurt me, I still think of him with great love and devotion.

How would you describe your father?

What are the things that you most love about your father?

When you close your eyes and think of your father, what is one vivid memory that comes to mind?

In what ways are you like your father?

In what ways are you different from your father?

What are some things you learned from your father that you have embraced?

What are some things you learned from your father that you have chosen to leave behind?

I want you to know you have a choice: you do not have to haul your parents' legacy into your life like that old dining room set your great-aunt left you in her will. If it makes you happy to eat at that table and sit in those chairs, by all means keep them. But if it doesn't, remember: You have options. You can hold on to the table and toss the chairs. Or lose the table and keep the chairs (perhaps reupholster the seats so they're more comfortable). And if you just plain hate the whole thing, get rid of it before you bring it into the house.

Just as your great-aunt's furniture might not suit your dining room, your parents' ways of living might not suit your life. You're not insulting your dead aunt by rejecting her old furniture, and you're not betraying your parents by living your life differently than they lived theirs; in fact, what you're doing is being true to yourself. I believe in the core of my being that you don't have to bring into your life anything that isn't working for you, nor are you fated to live out a future you had no part in creating. Each of us possesses the will to create her own legacy. It's all a choice.

Is this news to you? How does it make you feel to know that you can take the good, and the bad, from your parents' legacy and make your own life out of what you choose to keep? Is this notion freeing to you? Is it scary? How does this make you feel?

How do you feel about my statement that I feel each of us possesses the will to create her own legacy? Is this concept one you've claimed or embraced in your own life?

I do not believe that you have to feel guilty about carving your own life and your own legacy out of the one in which you grew up. As I've said earlier, choosing how to live your own life doesn't mean that you're betraying your parents by living your life differently than they lived theirs; you're simply being true to yourself. We cannot choose our genetics; our sex, how tall we'll be, and our race are all decided by our DNA. But at the same time, a great deal of our experience in this world *is* up to us.

The concept of redefining your legacy is something I am passionate about, especially when it comes to women, many of whom merely exist inside lives they neither chose nor contemplated. So many of us have dutifully reproduced our mother's or father's behaviors, duplicating our parents' patterns and manifesting a legacy that we, however unconsciously, feel obligated to fulfill.

To ask a perhaps blunt question:

Are you living someone else's life? Are you living the life you have chosen, or one that you feel has simply been passed down to you?

In what ways do you think you have unknowingly repeated family patterns in your own life? In what ways have you chosen to repeat these patterns?

Writing this book has required me to think about the choices I've made, and it has made me aware of the exhilarating power of living a life of my own choosing. I have never thought of myself as a victim of circumstance; rather, I examined the circumstances I was in, evaluated their usefulness in my life, and used them as a blueprint for how I would build the life I wanted. I always pictured myself as the one person and the only force besides God who I could count on to design the life I wanted to live, and make it a reality.

I knew I was meant to be a wife and mother, and I made it happen. I wanted a husband who didn't drink or gamble, and I made it happen. I wanted to take care of myself to remain vibrant and healthy for my family; and I made it happen (although I confess that the day I get rid of the treadmill just might be the happiest day of my life). And everything that has happened is the result of conscious choices that I made—some of which, I must tell you, were difficult to make and scary to live with. The bottom line, though, was that the thought of living a life I didn't want was much, much scarier than taking responsibility for choosing to create the life I did want.

When you think about the legacy of your family—about how they function (or *dys*function), it will probably bring lots of areas to mind: the ways in which they communicate, the ways that they show love and affection, the things that are most important to them, the way that they treat others, the way they treat and respect themselves, their goals in life, the way they view family. There are unlimited factors to consider, but all of these factors add up to your family legacy.

Now, specifically, what are some parts of that legacy that you want to refuse to bring into your own life? (This question is a hard question, I know, but one that I've found to be very important in the shaping of my own life. Take some time to thoughtfully consider what you want for your life.)

What are the things about your family's legacy that you know you want to continue to incorporate into your life?

I believe that in this life, we are defined not by the station in life into which we are born, nor by our pedigree, race, or religion, but by the choices we make. By choosing to live with passion and purpose, I have fashioned a rich and rewarding life—not because I'm special, or a genius, or born under a lucky star. Far from it.

What I've taken away from my childhood is the knowledge that my parents were only human and therefore fallible, and to think as they did and duplicate their actions would be to live their lives and not my own. I knew that to live my own life, I would have to pick and choose among the many examples my parents had set for me, and decide which to emulate and which to discard. I didn't hate my parents for the life we lived, not even for the bad and scary parts. But I also knew I would never, ever allow those nightmares to be part of my own family's life. I made the choice to embrace those parts of my parents' legacy that were good and wholesome, and to absolutely, categorically reject the rest.

In fact, that's what each of us has to do if we want to be truly autonomous, truly our own selves, and take our lives to the next level. And, contrary to the

> What I eventually came back to was that my father was not wholly a victim and that he bore some responsibility for abdicating control of his life. It was a stunning revelation, and it shaped the way I decided to live my own life. Today, I honor my father's memory by not letting anything control my life unless it's something I want in my life.

promises of our quick-fix culture, it doesn't happen overnight. It took years for me to work through my feelings about my parents, especially my father. What I eventually came back to was that my father was not wholly a victim and that he bore some responsibility for abdicating control of his life. It was a stunning revelation, and it shaped the way I decided to live my own life. Today, I honor my father's memory by not letting anything control my life unless it's something I want in my life.

That's what I meant earlier when I talked about dedicating my life to undoing the legacy of doubt, fear, and pain that accompanied my father's great love for us. My father taught me how good it felt to be really loved, and I vowed that when I had children someday, they also would feel really loved. But I also vowed to raise my children without the terrible uncertainty I grew up with. I promised myself that any children I brought into this world would grow up not only feeling loved, but also feeling supported by a consistent level of certainty that I never had as a child.

I am happy to say I have kept that promise, and I kept it both by the grace of God and the gift of free will. I kept this promise to my children by vowing not to marry a man who drank or gambled. And the fact that my children's father doesn't drink or gamble isn't a matter of chance, it's a matter of choice. It's no accident that Phillip embodies the values I wanted for the father of my children; the only reason he's the father of my children is *because* he embodies those values, and did when we were dating. That's why I chose him, and that's why I wanted him to choose me.

Do you feel that you have taken control of your life and the choices you've made? What are some things you are actively doing to ensure that you are following through with and supporting your own choices?

I keep coming back to this issue of making choices because I know so many people who don't realize they have the right to choose how they live, people who would be so much happier if only they would examine the connection between what they do and how their lives turn out.

For instance, what if, when Phillip and I were dating, he had told me that he loved me but couldn't promise that he would never stay out all night drinking, or never place a bet on a horse?

I would have moved on, that's what. Oh, yes, I would have.

As much as we love the people in our lives, the one thing we need to love even more is *ourselves*. Only we can know what we need to do to survive, to flourish, and harnessing ourselves to someone who brings chaos into our lives is not it. We can feel worthy; we can feel worth being loyal to.

As much as I wanted to marry Phillip, it wasn't about me holding onto him at any cost; it was about me holding onto me. I always wanted to be the most important part of my husband's life, whomever I married. If it wasn't going to be Phillip McGraw, it would be someone else. And whoever it was, no one and nothing would be more important to him than me.

Do you know that you are worthy—that you deserve to feel protected, loved, and important to the people in your life? You *are*! Do you feel that you deserve to have a life that treats you well, that is a life in which you can flourish and grow? You *do*! You deserve it! The value of *you* is not wrapped up in any legacy that you've been born into. You can make your own destiny. You can have a life that is fulfilling, that is what you've always dreamed of.

Do you feel that what I've just said is possible? Take some time to journal below about how reading this chapter has made you feel. Has it allowed you to feel hopeful? Has it opened doors of sadness or fear? Has it made you feel empowered?

There comes a time when you have to look deep within yourself and say, *As good a person as I am, as kind as I am, as loving as I am, that's still not enough. I have to respect myself and do what it takes to be able to live my life in a way that makes me proud.* As women, it is our responsibility to respect ourselves and do what it takes to live our lives in ways that make us proud. We need to live this truth every day.

Chapter Four

A HEART OF CLARITY AND CONVICTION:

Choosing to Go After What I Want

I believe that, in life, knowing what you want will get you only so far; the next step is getting it. And judging from my observations of human nature over the last half-century, it's the getting, not the wanting, that gives people trouble.

Especially women. Lord, I don't know what it is with us, but we sure seem to settle for less than we should. Considering that we are acknowledged to be the more intuitive half of the human race, we don't do much to press our advantage. Women are born with gifts of discernment that we could, and should, use to get what we want out of life. But too many of us decline to use our gifts, accepting what comes our

63

way rather than taking charge and making sure that what comes our way is what we want. I cannot count the women I know who feel they've been dealt a crummy hand, yet would rather play the cards they've been given than demand new ones. It's as if they're afraid the Cosmic Dealer will be angry with them if they ask for a better hand.

It's just the way life is: Each of us is born into a set of circumstances—a family drama, you might say—and assigned a role. We are expected to play this role not because our parents have it in for us, or our sisters and brothers are luckier, or because we were born under an unfortunate alignment of the planets.

> If you're a woman who is more comfortable reacting to life than acting upon it, I am here to tell you that you get what you ask for and that if you don't ask, you're going to end up settling for less than you want (and deserve).

Do you agree? Do you sometimes feel that you've just been dealt a crummy hand, but don't feel that you can do anything about it—or that you don't deserve to ask for something more? If you're a woman who is more comfortable reacting to life than acting upon it, I am here to tell you that you get what you ask for and that if you don't ask, you're going to end up settling for less than you want (and deserve).

Do you feel that you react to life rather than getting out there and being proactive? Why do you think you react the way you do?

In what areas of your life do you think you're settling for less than you deserve?

Is there something that you want right now in your life, but just aren't sure how to make it happen? What is it?

As soon as I know I want something to happen in my life, I start thinking and acting as if that much-desired thing is just around the corner, waiting for me to come and launch it into being.

It's one of the oldest sayings around, but I tend to believe that the Lord helps those who help themselves, and I've never hesitated to help myself to happiness when it's available. And it's available everywhere, if only people would see it. That's the thing: People don't see the potential they have for happiness because, on some level, they think they're as happy as they deserve to be, no matter how unhappy they are. To me, there's a huge difference between expecting happiness to come to you because you deserve it, and going out and getting the happiness you believe you deserve.

> To me, there's a huge difference between expecting happiness to come to you because you deserve it, and going out and getting the happiness you believe you deserve.

They say that luck is what happens when preparation meets opportunity, and I know it's true. A lot of things seem to go right for me, and it's not because I'm more deserving than other people; it's because I put a lot of energy into making things happen. I'm a great believer in the power of energy—the force that emerges when you set your mind to accomplishing something—and what happens when you use it as a catalyst: Things may not always turn out the way you imagined they would, but that's not the point. The point is to look inside yourself, identify what you need to be happy, and to put things in motion to secure that happiness.

Do you believe that you deserve to be happy? Why or why not?

Do you believe you can control your own happiness? What are some things that would make you happy right now?

How can you make those things happen?

I have said repeatedly that I believe that I was put on this earth to be Phillip's wife, and I believe that God meant for us to be together. But I also believe that God means for me to be an advocate for myself, both in my marriage and every other aspect of my life.

I followed Phillip when he left for the University of North Texas to start graduate school. We had been dating almost two years, and although we weren't ready to get engaged, we did want to be together. So Phillip and I decided I would move to Denton, get a job, and go to school at night.

> But I also believe that God means for me to be an advocate for myself, both in my marriage and every other aspect of my life.

I found a small apartment not too far from Phillip's place, and I also found a terrific job as the Unicom operator at Denton Municipal Airport. Plus I was taking college classes at night, so I was never bored. In the evenings Phillip and I would either meet at the university library or hang out at his apartment or mine and study. He was very focused on his schoolwork and didn't want anything to distract him from completing his Ph.D. And I understood and supported that 100 percent.

We had been there about a year when I began to feel strongly that I wanted to be married. Phillip and I spent all our nonworking time together, just like a married couple; only we lived in different places. There was no question about our commitment to each other, and it seemed to me that enough time had passed for us both to know what we were getting into. So I took a deep breath one night and put it out there.

"Phillip," I said, "we need to make a decision about where we're going with this. We've been together about three years now, and I would like to get married." He closed his book, cleared this throat, and looked into my eyes.

"Robin," he said, "I can't get married yet. I'm just not ready. I really feel I need to finish my education first. I can't stop like I did last time and go into business and all that. I'm so focused on finishing this program that I don't want to commit to you until I can give 100 percent to being married. I'm not going to get married until I can do that."

I let it sink in for a moment and then I spoke. "You know what?" I said. "I put my cards on the table and you chose not to play the hand. But now I know how you feel, and I'm out of here." I stacked up my books, put on my coat, and left.

It was probably the smartest thing I've ever done.

I was very serious about getting what I wanted and what I needed. And as much as I cared for him, I cared for myself just as much and I thought, *I am not going to be strung along here.* I was a really good girlfriend; I took really good care of him. I had devoted three years to showing him who I was and what life would be like if he chose me for his bride, and I wanted to know that we were going to get married. I thought this was perfectly reasonable (and I was right).

How does it make you feel when I say, "I believe God means for you to be an advocate for yourself"? Is this a new idea to you? How does it make you feel?

Like me, have you ever "put your cards out there," only to lose the hand? What did you do? Did you decide to wait and try to play again later? Did you get up and walk away from the table? Why do you think you reacted the way you did?

So Phillip and I broke up that night. But months later, he did ask me to marry him, and I said yes (big surprise). Not incidentally, I got what I wanted. And I had gotten it on my terms.

Have you ever gotten what you wanted on your own terms? What was the situation? How did it make you feel?

If you haven't had that experience, is there something you should go after right now—on your own terms?

My philosophy as a woman is, and always has been, that I would not settle for a loveless marriage, or subsist as a second-class citizen, or sacrifice my health to the latest fads, or live according to society's definition of what a woman should be. I insist, and have always insisted, on defining myself by the choices I make, and I started making them early in life.

Have you ever asked yourself the question, "Where do I draw the line? What do I really want out of life?" If not, dear friend, it's time you start asking. Because as I said earlier, I believe that if you don't ask for what you want in life, you probably won't get it. *How would you finish the statements below?*

I will not settle for . . .

I want the most important things in my life to be . . .

I may be reaching for the moon, but I really want . . .

I'm a big believer in knowing what you want and choosing to go after it—which is how I became the first childless Brownie troop leader in Waco, Texas.

Phillip was in graduate school and I was working during the day and taking classes at night. So, whereas I knew we'd have to wait a few years to have kids of our own, what was to stop me from having kids around who weren't my own?

This is exactly what I had in mind when I picked up the phone and called the local chapter of the Girls Scouts of America and told the woman who answered that I loved little girls and wanted to lead a Brownie troop. She was delighted. "How wonderful!" she said. "We always need leaders. What school does your daughter attend?"

"Actually, I don't have children," I said. "Not yet. I'm married and my husband's a graduate student in psychology and we're going to start a family when he graduates."

"You don't have children, but you want to lead a Brownie troop?"

"Yes, ma'am. I sure do."

"I don't believe we've ever had a request quite like yours. You'll have to come down to the office."

I had to go in for an interview so they wouldn't think I was a lunatic, and I had to prove that I really wanted to be a Brownie leader even though I didn't have any children. But I got a troop! I had eight little girls and they would all come to the house and I would run arts and crafts activities. The organization had guidelines we had to follow for the girls to earn their badges, so I did everything just so. At one of our meetings, I remember reading aloud from the official Girl Scout newsletter that kept leaders updated on programs and activities. And I got to the part about the annual Girl Scout jamboree, when they all get together for a few nights and go camping, and these little girls all started cheering and clapping because they were so excited.

Except I'd overlooked the fine print that said the overnight camping trip wasn't open to Brownie troops. The girls were devastated. It was so pathetic; one minute they were all cheering and the next they were sobbing around my kitchen table. So I said, "Okay, here's the deal; we'll have our own jamboree right here. We'll camp out in my back yard next weekend— How's that?" And don't you know, they were cheering again.

What I didn't realize was that Phillip would be out of town the following weekend, so I would have to run the jamboree on my own. But I had an idea. We lived next door to a wonderful couple, Ronnie and Diane. They were older and a bit like surrogate parents to Phillip and me. Ronnie's family owned a grave-digging business, so Ronnie was the person who would come out to the cemetery before a burial to dig the grave and set up a tent to shelter the family if the weather was bad. I called him and said, "Ronnie, I'm going to have a bunch of kids camped out in my backyard next weekend and Phillip won't be here; how do I set up a tent?"

"Don't worry," he said. "I'll handle it." And he put up a funeral tent to shelter my Brownies.

The following Saturday afternoon, eight cars pulled up to the house, and out popped eight little girls with sleeping bags, pillows, and Barbie dolls galore. I had planned all kinds of games and they were having a ball. Ronnie and Diane helped me feed them and when it began to get dark, the girls and I piled into our sleeping bags and snuggled up together. I read them stories and we had flashlights and marshmallows, and they eventually got drowsy and fell asleep.

I did too but was awakened a few hours later by the pitter-patter of raindrops that soon became a deluge. There I was, three o'clock in the morning under a funeral tent with eight groggy little girls, and it's lightning and they're squealing and I'm saying, "Girls, we're going to have to go into the house." Their sleeping bags were wet, so I ran to the linen closet, grabbed every sheet and blanket I owned (including the ones from our bed), and made pallets on the floor. Despite my best efforts, two girls were scared to death and crying, so I had to call their parents to come get them in the middle of the night. I was drenched and thought I would keel over with exhaustion. It was one of the best nights of my life.

The next morning dawned bright and clear, and I had six little angels sleeping on the living room floor in my little house; it was just adorable. I loved leading that Brownie troop because I got to do what I love to do: spend time with children and put my energies into making them happy.

I've thought about that Brownie troop many times since I last saw them (those little girls must be well into their thirties by now!) and what tickles me most about the whole experience is that I did it in the first place. I knew very well that troop leaders were typically the mothers of girls in the scouting program, but that didn't stop me. I knew that I wanted to work with children and that I'd have to find a part-time way of doing it. The Girl Scouts seemed like a good match so I pursued them, and we turned out to be perfect for each other.

Have you ever gone over and above to make something happen that was important to you? Write about it here. What did you have to do to make it happen? Was the experience harder than you thought it would be? Was it as rewarding as you'd hoped it would be?

When was a time that you felt total joy and elation over something you orchestrated?

I have a good life. Yes, I love the mosaic floors and crystal chandeliers in our house, but not any more than a certain pair of wooden barstools that graced our apartment when Phillip was in grad school. I'll never forget this. He was off working with his father for the weekend, and I decided I was going to do something fun with the apartment and surprise him when he got back. I had eight dollars left over from that week's budget to play around with, so I went to the store and bought a can of tangerine orange paint and a brush for five dollars, and a little ivy plant with the three dollars I had left. I came home to our bland little apartment with the beige walls and brown carpet and painted these two bar stools a bright tangerine color and set them next to the breakfast bar where they glowed like a Tahitian sunset. I took the green ivy and set it on the bar so it cascaded off the edge onto the seat of that shimmering barstool, and I thought it was the most beautiful thing I had ever seen.

And in many ways, it still is. Its preciousness transcended the eight dollars it cost me to create it, because it was born in my heart and made real by my hands. I imagined it and made it happen. To me there's nothing better.

Finish this thought: "To me, there's nothing better than . . ."

The sentence you just wrote represents something that is important to you, whether you realize it or not.

What do you think that statement says about you and what you want in life?

A lot of people have a great life, but they just don't see it. They choose to focus not on what they actually have but on what they believe they lack, and they miss what life is all about. Some people never have enough; no matter how devoted their mate is, they always wish he (or she) were fitter, richer, or more attractive. No matter how accomplished their kids are, they always think they could have won a bigger trophy or higher academic honor if only they'd tried a little harder. No matter how nice their car or how gracious their home, they always want a bigger or a fancier model. And while I firmly believe in striving for a good life, I also believe you've got to recognize when you've got it good and thank God for what you've got.

What are you thankful for? Journal here about these things.

Chapter Five

A Discerning Heart:

*What I Learned From My
Mother's Legacy of Love*

You never know when your life will change forever. One moment
your existence is tidy and ordered with everything and everyone in
its place; then a tornado blows through and life as you knew it lies
scattered around you, tattered and broken and making no sense at all.
That's what happened to me one Sunday morning over twenty years ago
when my mother collapsed and died of a massive heart attack while I was
talking to her on the phone. I had no warning, no time to prepare. All I
had was the sound of her voice and the incomprehensible realization, later,
that I would never hear it again.

After her death, what I remember most was a feeling of awe, because at that point, oddly enough, I wasn't as sad for myself as I was for my mother. I remember thinking, *What is wrong with me? I feel sorry for my loss but at the same time, I feel sorrier for hers.* My mother was such a precious woman; she loved her life. And all she wanted was for everyone to be happy.

That's what was causing me the worst anguish, the thought that she had been denied the chance to live the life she loved so much. She had been cheated out of what was most precious to her—time with the people she loved—and we had been cheated out of time with her. I replayed my mother's death over and over in my mind during the days that followed. First it made me cry, and then it made me think.

I was thirty-one years old, married for eight years, and the mother of a six-year-old boy. There was nothing in the world as precious to me as my husband and son. Just as my mother had always put her family's needs before her own, I had put my family's needs before mine. Like most mothers, I daydreamed about the milestones to come in Jay's life, and pictured myself beaming beside him as he grew stronger and taller and took his place in the world. In my mind I was always there, smiling and protecting him and making sure he was happy, just as my mother always did for us . . .

> It was then that I realized that loving your family and neglecting yourself are not the same thing; that, in fact, if a woman truly loves her family, she must not and will not neglect herself.

And then it would hit me. She was gone. My young son would grow up without his grandmother and perhaps forget what she looked like, or even that she existed. My life was immeasurably, profoundly diminished because she was gone. And she was gone because she didn't take care of herself.

It was then that I realized that loving your family and neglecting yourself are not the same thing; that, in fact, if a woman truly loves her family, she must not and will not neglect herself. I realized that my mother had martyred herself for the sake of her family, and we were all the poorer for it.

Often, as women we tend to put others' needs before our own. It seems that it happens almost unconsciously. Somewhere along the way, we begin to believe that the more sacrifices we make, the more we must be taking care of our families and friends. Is this happening in your life? Are you continually putting others' needs before your own?

How does it make you feel when I say that loving your family and neglecting yourself is not the same thing?

I know that this may be a hard concept to grasp, but I wholeheartedly believe it's true. You must make time to take care of yourself; otherwise you won't be the best you can be for others in your life. Do you set appropriate boundaries in your life that allow you to take care of yourself? Can you make the choice to say no to people or tasks in your life that keep you from putting yourself first?

What are some things that you could today to realign your priorities and to begin to take care of yourself?

I realized that it was too late to persuade my mother to take better care of herself, but it wasn't too late for me to learn from her tragedy and vow to take care of myself.

And I do. Ever since my mother died, I take care of myself as if my life depended on it. I do a breast self-exam in the shower several times a month. I go to the dentist every six months and have my teeth cleaned and checked. Every year I get a complete physical, a mammogram, and a Pap smear. And pardon me if I get on a soapbox here, ladies, but I'm talking to you. If you have not seen a doctor in the last year, please, please take a moment to think about yourself, about the gift of life that God has given you, and how little it takes for you to protect that gift. If you're not convinced, think about the people who love you—your husband, your children, your parents, your friends—and think about what their lives would be like without you. That's precisely the process I went through when my mother died: I pictured Jay having to grow up without me and Phillip having to raise him without me. I vowed I would always, always take care of myself—if not for my sake, then for theirs.

I am only five years younger than my mother was when she died. I've done the math and, according to my calculations (and by the grace of God), I believe I have thirty to forty years left. I have a lot of life left, and, as I see it, there is no excuse for me to do less than everything I can to be the best that I can be for a long, long time.

Are you in control of your health? What are the things you do to take care of yourself, physically and emotionally?

Do you struggle to make these things a priority in your life? What are some practical ways that you can "help" yourself to keep up the good things you are doing?

I also want to do whatever it takes to make myself feel good. When I was in my mid-forties, I started having hot flashes and went to see my gynecologist. I explained how I was feeling and she took some blood, saying she wanted to see me again the following week to go over the results.

When I returned, she entered the office with a grim look on her face. I was scared to death; what was wrong with me? She sat down at her desk, opened my file, and gave me the bad news.

"Robin, life as you know it is over—you're in menopause." She shook her head sadly as if to say, "Oh, you poor thing."

I was shocked. Menopause is a natural part of life that every woman will experience; why was she treating it like a tragedy? Admittedly, I didn't know much about the menopausal transition—yet—so I felt a bit overwhelmed and anxious at first. Still, it seemed to me that this part of my life didn't have to have such tragic overtones. The next thing I knew, she was handing me a stack of prescriptions.

"Fill these as soon as you leave here and get started on them right away," she said.

"What are these?" I said.

"Synthetic hormones. Trust me, you're going to need them." I looked through the slips of paper and tried to make out her handwriting—estrogen, progesterone, testosterone, DHEA, an antidepressant. I was floored.

"Do you give these to all your patients?"

"All of them going through menopause."

Now, I'm not a doctor, but it seemed odd to me that every menopausal patient would need precisely the same medications. I said so, and it seemed to hit a nerve.

"Trust me on this. You have no idea of what you're in for." *Not yet,* I thought, *but I will by this time tomorrow.*

"You know," I said, "I'd really prefer to do this more naturally. I go to an acupuncturist and see a homeopathic practitioner, and I think I'd like to visit with both of them before I start any prescription drugs."

She looked at me with real pity this time. "Look, Robin," she said, "if you don't take those drugs, you'll be back here in three months begging me to help you." And I thought, *Lady, I'm not the begging type.* I thanked her for her time and stuffed the prescriptions in my purse. I may have walked in a woman in menopause, but I walked out a woman on a mission.

> That day, I took charge of my health and made it my business to know my body and what it needed to thrive—and I urge every woman to do the same.

That day, I made a choice to turn that time of my life into a positive event and because of that choice, I believe today I am the healthiest I've ever been. That day, I took charge of my health and made it my business to know my body and what it needed to thrive—and I urge every woman to do the same.

Do you feel that you are in touch with what your body needs to function at its best? Do you trust your own instincts when it comes to your health? Why or why not?

If you aren't very confident in your instincts, what are some ways you can get to know your body and your health needs better?

Are you aware of your family's medical history? What are some health conditions you may need to keep an eye out for? How can you be proactive in protecting yourself from those conditions?

I don't take such vigilant care of myself because I think I can control everything; I do it because I know I cannot. My mother's death and other losses since then have taught me that no matter how organized and careful we are, from time to time life still has a way of bringing us to our knees. Like it or not, there are some things that cannot be controlled; not by me, not by anyone. Innocent children get hurt; hardworking adults lose their pensions; cities are blown away by hurricanes; and beloved wives, mothers, and grandmothers collapse and die of heart attacks while on the phone with their daughters. You can lament and carry on all you want to, but bad stuff happens to good people and there's not much any of us can do about it except choose how to respond. That is all any of us can do. And ultimately, it's all that matters.

I got my first inkling of this fairly early in my marriage. Phillip had this one relative I couldn't figure out. One day this person would act as if I were the best thing that had ever happened to the family, the next, as if I were an evil person who didn't deserve to live. So at family gatherings I'd come in all cheery and friendly and everything would be fine until the two of us would end up alone in a room together and this person would make a critical remark and leave me standing there, stung and reeling with confusion.

I took it very personally. Why was this person treating me this way? I wasn't about to make a scene; this was Phillip's family and I was the newest part of it. It was my job to be sweet, and (the way I saw it) it was Phillip's job to manage his family and make them treat me properly. So I would tell Phillip about these episodes and wait for him to say, "Robin, you are the kindest, most loving person on the planet, and no one has the right to treat you this way. I'm going to go over and straighten things out once and for all."

But he never said that. What he consistently said was, "You know what? This person did have the right to say that." And man, every time he said it, it felt like he'd slapped me. I felt like saying, *Now, wait a minute, buddy—you're supposed to be on my side!*

And he would look at me in this levelheaded way and say, "No, Robin. You're not going to convince me otherwise. This person had the right to say it. *But you have the right not to react to it.*" Every time Phillip said it I'd get mad at him, and I was mad a lot because this went on for a while. But the essence of what he was telling me, every time, was, *You can't control other people. You cannot control what they say, what they think, or what they do. People have the right to think and say whatever they want to. But you have the right not to take it to heart, and not to react.*

"When you allow a person's words to upset you, you're giving away your power," he said (in one of his early personal appearances as Dr. Phil). "You are giving someone else the power to control how you feel and how you think. You need to say, 'You have the right to say it and you have the right to think it. But I have the right to disagree; I have the right to not react; I have the right to continue to believe what I know is true.'"

I didn't like hearing it, but Phillip kept repeating it until one day a light bulb went on in my head and I realized, *He is neither betraying me nor agreeing with his relative; in fact, he completely disagrees. The reason he has this calmness about him is because he is dismissing this person's comments as nonsense, and he thinks I should do the same.*

Do you agree with Phillip—that you can't control other people and what they say, think, or do and that you have the right not to take their actions or words to heart? That you can choose not to react? How does what he says make you feel?

Phillip was right. And from that day forward, I have always known that what other people think of me or say about me ought not to influence what I know to be true about myself. To doubt myself because of others would be to hand over my power to them, and that is something I will not do. I never give my power away.

That's exactly what you do when you allow someone else's opinion of you to affect your opinion of yourself: You're giving away your power. And I say, don't do it. It doesn't matter how convinced of your flaws your detractors may be; if you allow other people to erode your good opinion of yourself, you're giving them power over you. This family member truly felt righteous about judging me harshly, but what I failed to see at the time was that the judgment was more about that person than it was about me. Some combination of irrational thoughts, distorted perceptions, and unknowable events in that person's life motivated those behaviors. Ultimately (and ironically), it had nothing to do with me. The moment I accepted this person's right to be conflicted and in turmoil, I was able to restore my own equanimity. I now enjoy a warm relationship with this person because I made a decision to allow in only the positive aspects of the relationship and to reject the bad ones. I could not control this person, but I could control myself.

How do you usually respond when you feel someone treats you badly?

Does the way you react cause you to give up your power or to retain it? Why?

The next time that you have an unpleasant interaction with someone, what can you do to retain your power over the situation?

I have come to see that within every event lies a realm of possible responses, and by choosing among them I define who I am. And I'm not talking only about grand, life-changing events; I'm talking about everyday happenings and interactions, like the ones you get into with the people you love and live with, and the one I got into with my husband not long after my mother's death.

When I finally finished the heartbreaking task of writing thank-you notes to those who had taken such good care of me after her death, I put a stamp on each one, stacked them up, put them in a little bag, handed them to Phillip, and said, "If you'll mail these for me tomorrow at the office, I can now start living my life without my mother." And he took the bag and said, "Of course I will."

One morning about three weeks later while Phillip was in the shower, I picked up his tennis bag and swung it onto the bed. I gathered up his tennis clothes and was putting them into the bag when I felt something bulging in from a side pocket. I unzipped the pocket and reached down in there, and what did I find but the bag full of thank-you notes.

My heart broke. It was as if my mother had died all over again.

I started crying. And as I stood there weeping and missing my mother, Phillip walked into the room. He stared at me and he stared at those notes and he stood there with the most horrified look on his face.

"Oh . . . my . . . God," he said, his voice barely a whisper. "I forgot to mail them." I was really sobbing now.

"I thought they knew! I thought they knew! I've seen these people, Phillip, in the store, and on the street, and I never said a word of thanks to them because I thought they'd gotten my cards! I thought they knew!" The poor man just stood there. His face was the color of ashes.

I was hurt, I was angry, I was in pieces all over again. Not only had I felt good about thanking so many people for comforting me, but writing to them about my mother and imagining them reading what I'd written was a huge part of my healing process. I had seen these people around town, and it had given me comfort to know that there had been an exchange between us, that I had properly acknowledged their condolences, expressed my gratitude for their caring, and left them knowing a little bit more about my mother after her death than they had known when she was alive. At the time, I felt I was repaying their kindness by writing, with my own hand, anecdotes about what a wonderful woman my mother had been. Then when I'd see these people in town I would imagine we shared a bond and think, *We are some of the lucky ones, you and I, because we share this secret of how extraordinary my mother was, and how great a loss it is that she is gone.*

But now that illusion was also gone; there was no knowledge between us, no secret shared. I felt like one of those palm trees you see on The Weather Channel hurricane updates, blasted about by gale-force emotional winds that could knock me over at any moment. I felt devastated and shocked and sad and angry.

I also felt betrayed. How could this matter so little to him? How could this man think he knew me and not realize the value of these notes? How could he think he loved me if he couldn't remember to do this one hugely important thing?

I looked up and Phillip was standing in the same place quietly saying, "I'll cancel my patients and I'll spend the whole day . . . I'll call them . . . I'll make a list and call them. I'll get their phone numbers, I'll call everyone—no, I'll go see them, that's what I'll do, I'll hand-deliver the notes. Just give them to me and I'll go right now, Robin, I'll do whatever it takes. Please, please let me make this up to you."

And something melted inside me and I thought, *Bless his heart.* This precious man is devastated, just as I am, and suddenly I knew that his feelings were more important to me than the feelings of the people who hadn't received the notes. I thought, *He is suffering so much more for not mailing the notes than they are; what do I gain by punishing him with my anger? What benefit do I derive by making him suffer more?*

This was a powerful moment for me personally and a pivotal one in our marriage. I had the right to rant and rave and scream and yell and make Phillip feel horrible. *I had the right to behave that way.* Instead, I seized the opportunity to show him who I actually was: a compassionate and forgiving woman who loved him, no matter what, and who would forgive him, no matter what.

So I looked into his sad, sad eyes and blotted my own with my sleeve. "I know you didn't do it on purpose," I said. "We'll mail them today and they'll get them tomorrow. I love you and I know you love me, and I know you didn't do it on purpose." And the look of gratitude on his face showed me how fortunate he felt. I think of that moment as the one when Phillip learned that my love for him and commitment to him was stronger than any mistake he might make. I believe that was the moment he learned he could trust me, and he has never forgotten it.

I believe in forgiveness. I believe that, just as God promises to forgive us, He wants us to forgive one another.

When someone has wronged and hurt you, does forgiveness toward that person come easily for you or do you struggle with holding grudges? How do you usually handle the situation?

Is there someone in your life who you need to forgive for hurting you? How might practicing forgiveness towards that person change your relationship with him or her? How might it change you?

Every day offers a chance to choose either anger or understanding, bitterness or acceptance, darkness or light. And the choices we make reveal the stuff we're made of. It is an option every woman has, if only she will use it. It's your choice.

Chapter Six

A WIFE'S HEART:

Choosing To Do Whatever Makes My Husband Happy

I am in the audience at the *Dr. Phil* show every day, and I have been since it first aired four years ago. I absolutely love it; I wouldn't miss it for the world. I love being there because this show—the work my husband does in that time—is his life's passion. It is his calling and he has asked me to be there with him and for him. I love that he wants me there and I love that I can be there. The *Dr. Phil* show isn't just Phillip's job; it's part of the fabric of our lives.

If there's one thing I've learned in the many years we've been married, it is that in a relationship, each person needs to actively be on the lookout for what the other needs. I think the success of a marriage is in large part based on the willingness of each partner to do what it takes to meet the other's needs. And in my experience, men are pretty obvious about letting you know what they need; we women just have to learn to read the signals.

> I think the success of a marriage is in large part based on the willingness of each partner to do what it takes to meet the other's needs.

Men are different from us; they're not going to take us by the hand and say, "Sweetheart, I want to talk to you about these feelings I've been having," and beg us to do this, that, or the other thing—forget that. What they are going to do is get out of the shower twenty minutes before you're due to be somewhere and say, "So, what are you thinking of wearing tonight?" It doesn't matter that your outfit is laid out on the bed alongside seven others you've already rejected and they're all long, dressy, and black. Because he's not really asking you what you're going to wear, he's asking you to tell him what *he's* going to wear. It's a guy code they use to let us know that they need help without actually asking for it.

It seems so strange, but in relationships, we often talk in "code" to one another. Why do you think we do that? Can't we just say what's on our minds? I think we do it because we are often afraid to just come out and say what we need or want from each other.

Are you comfortable asking those in your life what they need or what they want from you? Why or why not?

Are you comfortable telling others the things that you need or want? If the answer is no, why do you think that is difficult for you?

I'm often astonished at the number of women who either don't pick up the signals their men are sending out or, even worse, pick them up loud and clear and choose to ignore them, as though it would diminish their power to help out.

I once knew a woman who was always at odds with her husband. They didn't argue or yell, but it was as if she had a constant, underlying need to get him before he got her. I couldn't figure it out; I never heard him speak unkindly or disrespectfully to her, and he seemed like a very decent man. Still, his happiness was never very high on her list of priorities.

I remember she was at the house once when her husband was away on a fishing trip, and she was talking about how he loved to meet up with these old friends every year, and they would rent a boat and spend a week hanging out and being guys together. She said he'd been gone a week and was coming home that afternoon. I looked at the clock and saw that it was past three o'clock.

"You'd better get going," I said, "or you won't be there when he gets back."

"Oh, that's okay," she said.

"But don't you want to be there when he gets home?"

"No, not really."

"What?"

"Sure, he'd like me to be sitting there when he gets home so he can drag in his cooler and show me all the fish he caught. If he's so interested in being with me, why does he need to go away? If he's going to go away for a week, fine, but I'm sure as heck not going to be sitting there when he walks in, because that's exactly what he wants."

Was she kidding me? She apparently knows what he wants, what he needs, what he likes, and she's not going to do it *on purpose?* What's up with that?

If your mate lets you know what he wants and you use that information to hurt him, you've got to ask yourself why you are in the relationship in the first place. Here's this woman doing the opposite of what her husband wants so he won't think he can control her, whereas if she would wait for him to come home, crawl up in his lap and flirt with him, she'd have him hooked better than anything in that cooler of his. I just sat there thinking, *Whoa—if my husband told me exactly what it would take to make him happy and I didn't use that information, how stupid would that be?* (Answer: *Very.*)

There are lots of different ways to respond when we encounter conflict or tension in our closest relationships, some healthy and some not.

When you're in conflict with someone close to you, how do you usually respond? Do you go quiet and shut that person out, hoping he or she will get the point? Do you get loud and vocal? How do you respond and why do you think you respond the way you do?

As in the story about this particular woman, sometimes we deliberately hold back from the ones we love in order to get back at that person or to protect ourselves in some way. Carefully consider this:

Are you deliberately denying someone in your life something that he or she needs or wants? Do you feel that someone is deliberately denying you something you need or want? If either question describes you, what can you do to turn the situation around?

Phillip may not be perfect, but there's no question that he's the perfect man for me. And I will love him and stay with him and be a good wife to him forever, no matter what. I know this because we had a conversation right before we got married, and we decided that this marriage was forever, that we were never, ever going to divorce. We would never even talk about divorce. We were going to do whatever it took to make the marriage work because we didn't want to live in uncertainty, wondering, is this the day that he walks out? Is this the one thing that's going to make him so angry that he leaves? Or, from his point of view, is this the one thing that's going to make her say, "I've had it—I'm out of here!"? When we both made the commitment and decided that there was nothing, ever, that was going to make either of us leave, it took a lot of pressure off both of us.

You might think it would be the other way around—that a woman and man who were young, still in school, and with little money, might feel anxious that they had sworn to stay together no matter how disappointing things turned out. But for us, commitment granted freedom to the marriage: freedom for both of us to not only be our true selves, but to speak the truth about who we were and what we needed without worrying that either one of us would walk out over a thoughtless remark or a stack of unmailed thank-you notes in a tennis bag. For us, commitment was liberating, not confining, because it promised certainty and continuity that was both comforting and necessary. For me, because of the kind of home I'd come from, it was no less than sacred. And to this day, the most significant aspect of the commitment is that each of us chose to make it, freely and without pressure.

> For us, commitment was liberating, not confining, because it promised certainty and continuity that was both comforting and necessary.

One cannot put a price on the value of a safe, secure relationship.

Have you ever experienced this kind of secure, trusting relationship with someone? What was it like? How did you feel being in that relationship?

On the flip side, there's nothing worse than being in an unstable, vulnerable relationship.

Have you ever experienced that kind of relationship? How did you feel being in that relationship? What did you learn and how can you avoid being in those kinds of relationships in the future?

Have you ever made the decision to be completely committed to a relationship? Have you ever run away from a committed relationship? Do you agree with me, that commitment really equals freedom? Why or why not?

I realize that you may be reading this and thinking, *I made a commitment to someone, and I truly believed it meant "forever." But it didn't work out. The relationship failed. So where does that leave me?*

Friend, let me just say that beyond the pain of a failed relationship, there is a choice. A choice to make decisions for yourself in the future that lead you into secure and healthy relationships.

Ask yourself, what have you learned from that failed relationship? How can it influence future relationships in my life?

I believe that good marriages aren't born, they're made—and they're made over time by an ongoing process of loving, unselfish negotiation. It's funny; people are forever asking me how Phillip and I have managed to be married for thirty years and still be happy. They think we have some sort of mysterious secret; when I tell them that we've done it by negotiating our differences, they look almost disappointed. *Negotiate?* they say. That sounds so, so . . . unromantic.

Well, hello! Who ever said marriage is romantic? Marriage is about partnership, sharing, cooperation, and compromise. Sure, romance is in there, too, but it tends not to surface unless the other components are in place. And they're not going to fall into place easily and peacefully all the time. Sometimes you have to advocate for yourself in a relationship, which means figuring out what your needs are in a given situation and having the conviction to be honest with your partner about it.

Here's an example. My sister Cindi invited me to her house for the weekend. She was still married then and the girls were very young, so it was easier for me to go up to Oklahoma—she lived not far from the Texas border—than it was for her to come down to my place. So I called Phillip and told him that I was going to visit my sister for the weekend and I invited him to come along. We weren't married yet, and between his graduate school classes, studying, and teaching assistant job, I didn't see him that much. So I thought it would be fun to hang out with my sister and my nieces for a few days. And he said, "Sure, I'll go."

About an hour later he called back. "I've got to thinking," he said, "and you know what? I am so busy and there's so much I can be doing here, and it's not my thing to sit around and visit and have girl time. I know you want to have a visit with Cindi, so why don't you go by yourself and I'll stay behind? You know I love to spend my free time playing tennis on the weekends and I can't do that there, so . . . unless you really want me to go for some reason, why don't you just go do your thing, and I'll stay here and do my thing? We'll see each other when you get back. Okay?"

And I said, "See you Monday."

He wasn't putting me down or letting me down; we were only dating at the time, after all, and he was under no obligation to accompany me on a trip whose sole purpose was for me to visit my family. Nor was he implying that I should not go and instead remain in town to be with him. He was merely asserting his preference for the weekend and being honest with me about how he would rather spend his time. It had nothing to do with me, and it had everything to do with him and what he needed to do that weekend to feel responsible, studious, and satisfied with himself.

Now, I know many women would be hurt if their boyfriends turned down an invitation to spend a weekend at their sister's house. They'd work it out in their heads that he didn't really love them, or didn't like their families, or didn't care about their feelings, when they should have been thanking the guy for being honest enough to tell them how he really felt. I actually felt relieved that Phillip told me he didn't want to go, because if he'd come along and been miserable, it would have ruined my weekend. And I'll always be grateful to him because, by being honest about what he wanted to do, he liberated me to be honest about my preferences, too. And I have been, throughout our marriage.

What would have been your initial response to Phillip if you were me and he had said he didn't want to go visit my family for the weekend? Were you surprised by my reaction? Why or why not?

Do you think it sounds unromantic to say that marriage and other relationships are often successfully managed by negotiation? Have you found this negotiation principle to be true in your life? If so, what tactics work for you?

Just because Phillip and I came together as a couple doesn't mean that we love all the same things. I never understand it when I hear a woman say she's not going to do something she enjoys because her husband won't do it with her, because that means you have to give up part of yourself for as long as you're married. As I said earlier, you're not the same person as your husband; why expect him to like all the same things you do? I love girl time. I love spa days. Phillip wouldn't go to a spa for the day if you held a gun to his head, but he encourages me to do it (go to the spa, not hold a gun to his head). To this day, he urges me to go see my sisters when he senses I'm missing them. He is supportive of anything I want to do that brings me joy, and I am supportive of anything he does that brings him joy.

That's why I insist that he play tennis every day. I still get up in the morning and pack a bag with everything he needs so he can play tennis on his way home from the studio. And he does, every single day that the weather is good (and in LA, it usually is). He's always played tennis after work, and I've always encouraged him to do it.

Over the years a lot of people have said, "I can't believe that it's okay with you that he goes straight to the tennis court for two hours after work." And I always say, "Who am I to tell him he can't do that?" I mean it: He works hard all day, and afterward he needs to work out and sweat and breathe and get rid of his stress. He wants that. That's who he is, and I don't want him to give up an important part of himself because he's married to me. In a marriage, you have to do what works.

Do you feel it's OK to have different interests than your partner? How do you balance between time away from each other and time together?

Do you feel resentful toward someone in your life because they have different interests than you? Why? How can you change the way you respond to that situation?

As I said before, it's all about doing whatever it takes to make your partner happy. That is true for husbands and wives alike, but I'm focusing on the wife's part of the deal for obvious reasons. Phillip has never invaded my motherly turf. I don't think he ever changed a diaper or woke up in the middle of the night with a crying child because that's the way I wanted it. He did wake up once and wander over to Jay's crib when he was crying and I shooed him back to bed because his job was to work during the day to support the family; mine was to care for the family so he could focus on work. That was our agreement when we got married, and we were both satisfied with the terms. Phillip takes his work very seriously—that man loves working more than anyone I know—and I take my work seriously, too.

> Nothing means more to a woman than when her family lets her know they appreciate all she's doing for them.

Phillip has never complained about being the sole breadwinner in our family, and I have never felt resentful, put-upon, or exploited because I was responsible for the childcare and housework: Those are things that I am good at, and things I love to do. Had I felt overwhelmed or unhappy at any point I would have renegotiated the terms of our agreement. But I have always felt content in the role I chose to play in this life and this family—even when times were hard—because my husband has always shown his appreciation for what I do.

Appreciation is a big component of a successful marriage. I hope that every underappreciated woman who reads this will circle that last sentence with a DayGlo® marker and put it where her husband or kids can see it. Nothing means more to a woman than when her family lets her know they appreciate all she's doing for them. And every woman does a lot: Whether she's a working mother or home full-time, it's the rare woman who isn't the heart of her home, and her worth is beyond reckoning. I know plenty of women who did not choose, as I did, to make full-time careers of raising their families—a lot of them work on the *Dr. Phil* show—and who work demanding, full-time jobs and then go home to husbands and children and housework galore. No matter how much money they bring in, there's nothing more important in these women's lives—or in any woman's life—than feeling she is special and irreplaceable to the people she loves.

How are the roles of your closest relationships defined in your world? Were these definitions a conscious role on your part? How do you feel about these roles? Does anything need adjusting?

Do you feel appreciated in your closest relationships? If not, what do you need in that area? How can you communicate what you need to your family?

Are you showing your partner the appreciation he deserves? How do you express that to him?

The simple act of turning your consciousness away from your own inner world to connect with your partner's is a great gift to a relationship; in fact, it's the essence of relationship. You've got to be willing to put energy into listening to your partner—not just hearing, but really listening—so you can pick up signals he's sending out about what he needs to be happy. And you've also got to be willing to send out some signals yourself that enable your partner to make *you* happy.

> The simple act of turning your consciousness away from your own inner world to connect with your partner's is a great gift to a relationship; in fact, it's the essence of relationship.

I was once talking to a woman who was complaining that her birthday had just passed and once again her husband had failed to give her a pair of diamond stud earrings that she wanted very badly. I asked her if she had told him that she wanted the earrings and she said, "No, but I shouldn't have to; he should know what I want by now. And besides, I wanted him to surprise me."

"Well," I said, "how can the poor man surprise you if you don't tell him what you want?"

Yes, Phillip surprises me with special gifts, but he knows I will like them because I've usually made a point of saying so. I don't just say I like certain things so that he will buy them for me, but I certainly have nothing to lose by saying something. In doing so, I give Phillip the information he needs to make me happy, and he gives me the gift of paying attention. That is something that Phillip and I have always given each other: we pay attention.

How do you put energy and time into cultivating connections with the important people in your life? What are some things that you can do to strengthen those relationships and begin to pay more attention? How can those in your life develop a deeper connection with you? Can you share that information with them?

Chapter Seven

A Confident Heart, or When I'm Right, I'm Right

Every woman is different, but there is one thing that works for all of us—and that is confidence. There is nothing unfeminine about confidence; in fact, many men will tell you there is nothing more attractive than a woman who knows her own mind and stands by what she thinks. When you are confident, you tell the world that you will not be taken advantage of. You teach the men in your life to treat you with dignity and respect, and you set an example of what a strong, independent woman can accomplish in this world (and what a blessing she is).

As women, we are trained from childhood to be good little girls, to smile and charm and be agreeable. But acting agreeable is not a virtue when you know in your heart that you absolutely, positively *disagree* with the people around you. If you smile and nod and go along with the crowd—or the authorities—when your heart is telling you otherwise, you are betraying your true self and denying your God-given powers of discernment.

Do you feel that confidence is an unfeminine quality? Why or why not? Do you consider yourself a confident person?

Growing up, how were you taught, either directly or indirectly, that a woman should behave?

Did the instruction you received include having great respect for yourself and your own opinions and instincts? Explain.

As a woman, what do you believe are some of your "God-given powers of discernment"?

Who are some confident women you admire? What do you admire about them?

Most mothers have knowledge, stronger than intuition or anything in a book. You know your child, you know when something isn't right, and you know that you must do something about it. Most new parents have had an episode with their children, a close call that turned out well but was scary for a while. It stays with you because the feelings it provokes are so powerful that they remain vivid decades later, well after the child is grown.

> You can't stand by passively and ignore your maternal, womanly instincts in a situation with your children or any other kind of challenging situation.

I have learned from those experiences we've had, and what I learned was to trust my instincts and not back down when I know I'm right. It is my calling to take care of my children; I am their mother, and I believe that I am called by God to love and protect them with every breath I have in me. If I have to make a fuss, fine; if people get annoyed with me, so be it. Ruffling a few feathers is a small price to pay for saving my child's life.

Now, I don't want to give the medical profession a bad rap. But you have to stand up for yourself. You can't stand by passively and ignore your maternal, womanly instincts in a situation with your children or any other kind of challenging situation. You can't let anyone tell you something about anything in your life without thinking, feeling, and acting in accordance with your instincts and knowledge. It's not about being stubborn, hardheaded, or close-minded; it's about listening to yourself and trusting what you hear.

> What I am urging is that you become an active participant in the creation and maintenance of your own well-being, and that of your loved ones.

It's not always easy to stick up for yourself. People in authority can be intimidating, especially when they're not accustomed to being challenged. And there's always a chance that you'll raise a ruckus, only to find out you were wrong and end up looking like an idiot. But I'd rather risk looking like an idiot than feel like one for being too intimidated to stand up for me and mine.

I am not urging you to be mistrustful or hostile toward others. What I am urging is that you become an active participant in the creation and maintenance of your own well-being, and that of your loved ones. Sometimes that requires pushing back. And I believe too many people are content to merely go along to get along.

Do you trust your own instincts? Are you confident enough in those instincts that you will vehemently defend them? Why or why not?

Are you afraid to make a fuss or ruffle feathers? In what situation might it be appropriate to do so?

It's not enough, for example, to show up at the clinic, wait your turn (usually far too long), and spend your three minutes with the physician (or physician's assistant or nurse practitioner) listening passively and filling the prescription you may get on your way out. You have to be fully present at the encounter, which means not just listening but interacting with the person who is treating you.

I make a point of asking questions. If a physician says something I don't understand, I ask what he's talking about. If I have read or heard something that I'd like to have confirmed or debunked, I'll raise the issue. If the doctor seems to be missing something that I consider important, I'll bring it up. And if he—or she—seems to be ignoring something I'm saying or dismissing something I'm feeling, I let him or her know, politely but firmly, that I am a force to be reckoned with. Don't be intimidated because you don't have a professional degree: You don't need one to be knowledgeable about your own body, mind, or family. I am not a doctor, lawyer, or teacher, but that doesn't stop me from reading everything I can get my hands and eyes on, and educating myself about issues that concern me and my family.

I am not afraid to question authority. I am not willing to give my power away to anybody just because she sits behind a desk or wears a white coat. I believe I am accountable for whatever happens to me and to those under my care, and that this is true for all of us. I believe it is my responsibility to stand up for what I believe is right, no matter how uncomfortable it feels. Moreover, I believe that is what God wants me to do. He blessed me with the intelligence to think for myself and parents who taught me to trust my judgment, and I believe I would be squandering these gifts from above if I did not put them to good use here on earth.

Now let me make something perfectly clear: I am not saying that I'm always right. We all make mistakes, including me, but when you know you're right, you're doing yourself a disservice if you don't stick up for yourself.

How do you feel when you are in conflict with someone in a position of authority? Do you readily stand up or question those people when you disagree with them? Do you back down? Why do you think you react the way you do?

Have you ever stood up for something only to be wrong? What happened and how did you respond?

Have you ever stood up for something, and you were right? What happened and how did you respond?

You've got to listen to that voice inside you that tells you the truth. It's quiet and steady and certain of its rightness because it comes from a deep part of you, the part of you that simply knows. Each of us has that deep inner wisdom that comes from our life experiences, but we don't always trust it enough to obey it.

It's very important that women not be afraid to stand up for themselves. Too many women are willing to abdicate their responsibility as mature, thinking adults because they have been taught that they should defer to authority, especially when the authority is a man. We women can be a little too quick to abandon our inner wisdom when someone in a position of power contradicts it.

You've got to listen to that voice inside you that tells you the truth. It's quiet and steady and certain of its rightness because it comes from a deep part of you, the part of you that simply knows. Each of us has that deep inner wisdom that comes from our life experiences, but we don't always trust it enough to obey it.

Stand up for yourself. It isn't necessary to be a bully; you don't have to be mean. But when it comes to looking out for yourself, the one who is ultimately responsible is *you*. And I'm not just talking about medical emergencies and business disputes where the stakes are obviously, glaringly high. I'm also talking about everyday situations when you're not being treated as you would like to be, but you let it slide because you don't want to embroil your family, friends, or spouse in a conflict. There's always a temptation to ignore these episodes, telling yourself that they're no big deal and not worth fighting over when, in fact, you don't have to approach every difference of opinion as a conflict.

Why do you think it's sometimes hard to listen to your inner voice and to trust your experiences and wisdom?

How can you be confident and assertive in a situation without being mean and rude?

Ladies, have confidence in yourself. Trust your own judgment. When you know you're right, don't let anyone tell you otherwise. Don't stop; don't back down. Stand up for yourself and defend what you know is true: If you don't, no one else will.

Chapter Eight

THE HEART OF MY HOME

Like everyone else, I am not one person but many. I am a daughter to parents no longer living; a sibling of five who bear scars of growing up in a loving but chaotic household. I am a wife to a man whose heart I hold in my hands; and a mother to sons whose lives I hold dearer than my own. I am a sister-in-law, a daughter-in-law, and a mother-in-law. And above all things and embracing all things, I am the heart of my home.

Aren't all women the hearts of their homes? Whether we live alone or in a household spanning three generations, whether we work outside the home as well as within it or stay at home full-time, it's the women who make sure there's food in the fridge, curtains on the windows, sheets on the beds, and a hug for whoever needs it. With few exceptions, it's a woman's spirit that brings a house its warmth, brightens its shadowy corners, and provides those who live there with a soft place to fall. There are as many ways to do this as there are women: We all have our own unique way of being in this world and creating the joy and warmth that make a house a home.

How would you define your role as the heart of your home?

What are three words that describe what you want your home to be like, for those living there and for those who are guests in your home?

What are some tangible ways you can create the kind of home you've just described?

I like to try to make life fun for my family. When the boys were little and Phillip and I were going out of town—Phillip traveled a lot to do seminars, and sometimes I would go with him—we would leave them with their grandparents, who spoiled them rotten. Still, just to make sure they didn't miss us too much, I would get little bags and if we were going to be gone Monday, Tuesday, and Wednesday, I'd write "Monday a.m.," "Monday p.m.," and so on. I'd put a little note in along with something fun—a Hot Wheels car, a piece of gum, a sucker, whatever they loved—and they'd get to open them when they woke up in the morning and before they went to bed. That was my way of letting them know that there were times when Mom and Dad needed to go away together, but that we were always loving them and thinking of them.

I also made a big deal about holidays. In spring, I would buy little napkins decorated with Easter eggs and chicks, write a message on the napkin, and stick it in their lunch boxes so they'd get a loving note from me while they were at school. Every Valentine's Day I would buy red heart-shaped balloons and tie them to their chairs before they came down for breakfast. On their birthdays I took lipstick and wrote messages on their bathroom mirror while they were sleeping, so they'd wake up, go in to brush their teeth, and get a surprise.

I would often try to find ways to surprise them. On the days Jay had a game after school, I would drive out there and bring him a hot lunch because the school he went to had no kitchen, and he'd get hungry during the game if he hadn't had a substantial lunch. I would serve the boys' favorite dinner on game days and surprise them with their favorite dessert. Sometimes I'd bake a chocolate-chip cookie cake (get a roll of cookie dough, press it into a pan, presto!), put their jersey number on it in M&Ms, and let them have it when we got home from the game. They loved that because not only did it make game days feel special to them, it let them know that I thought they were special too.

Maya Angelou says, "If you only have one smile in you, give it to the people you love. Don't be surly at home, then go out in the street and start grinning 'Good morning' at total strangers."

How does this quote make you feel? Do you give your smiles to your family, first and foremost?

As the heart of your home, what are some things that you can do to make your loved ones feel special and that they are important to you?

What is one thing you can do for someone today to show him or her your love and appreciation?

I have always chosen to cultivate a spirit of happiness in our home. It didn't get there by itself; I made it that way. It is not enough that I am happy in myself; I choose to spread a spirit of joy and fun to the family. If I don't, Phillip and the boys might not have it, and it's exactly what they need.

If I weren't around, my husband would probably work all the time, and he's not the only one. I often hear women talking about how their husbands have forgotten how to leave work behind, let go, and have fun. A lot of these are working women, so they understand how difficult it is to juggle professional and personal responsibilities. Still, they seem to be better at making time for fun than their husbands, and are at a loss as to how to help their husbands do the same. I know what it's like to be married to a man who loves to work, and I'd like to pass on something I've learned: One of the best things women can do to make their husbands happy is to be happy themselves. Phillip cannot stand it if he thinks I'm unhappy about something, and I know it brings a real peace to his life—

and to our household—to know that I am just where I want to be, doing just what I want to do.

How does it make you feel to know that one of the best things you can do for those in your home is to be happy yourself?

What are some things you are doing to cultivate your own happiness?

I feel grateful for the opportunity I've been given to reach out through these pages and connect with you. For that is how women are: first we connect with our hearts, then with our minds. And writing these words has made me even more aware of the women who have touched my heart and mind, and, in so doing, nurtured my soul.

I think of my blessed mother-in-law, whose sturdy, constant strength and love eased the anguish I felt when my beloved mother died. Grandma Jerry is in her eighties now, and of all the gifts she's given me, perhaps the greatest of all is her relentless affirmation of my importance in her son's life. She validates me as a wife, and not only does that make me feel good, it also shows me how to be the kind of mother-in-law I want to be.

And then there's my sister Cindi, whose courage and grace in the face of unspeakable suffering have inspired me with awe. Cindi and her boyfriend were driving to the airport early one morning when a maniac on an overpass dropped a jug of sulfuric acid through the windshield of their car, studding her with glass, catastrophically burning her face and body, and shattering her life. Even today, more than five years later, it's hard for me to discuss the event without wanting to scream and shake with rage about the injustice of it all. But Cindi does not.

My amazing sister chooses to see the experience not as a vicious attack against her but precisely for what it was: a random, barbaric act directed at everyone in general and no one in particular by a human being with a profound indifference to human suffering. Cindi knows there is nothing she could have done to avoid or prevent the catastrophe; it was out of her control. She believes that as much as she has suffered (and she has, horribly), there are people who suffer more than she, and for just as little reason. She never felt sorry for herself or expressed grief over her disfigurement. She never cursed the person who did this to her—although, Lord knows, the rest of us did. I was proud of her for not caving in to despair and for choosing forgiveness instead. In so doing, she reclaimed her life from horror and insisted on her God-given right to live out her time here on earth.

Who are the people in your life you really appreciate—those who make you feel stronger, happier, loved? What about each of them do you appreciate most? How do they make you a better person?

When I think of my sister's extraordinary grace, I am reminded of God's continuing and eternal presence in our lives. I said at the beginning of this book that I believe we were put on this earth to enjoy lives of joy and abundance. That is what I wish for Cindi and myself, and what I wish for you, and for all women. My wish is for you to perceive, as I do, the presence of God within us and around us and to feel the love He feels for all of us. I have total peace in my heart because I know I can turn to God at any time and ask for help. I know I can. That's why before I get out of bed every morning and before I go to sleep every night, I thank God for all that He has blessed me with.

What are some ways in which you feel God has blessed and enriched your life?

What are you thankful for today?

There will always be people who want to tell you who you should be and what you should do, but no one can tell you how to live your life because there is no one quite like you. Look inside yourself with open eyes and see who's really in there —not your mother or your father, not your husband or your children, but you. Go deep, really deep, beyond the labels of wife and mother, daughter and sister, until you find the essential woman inside, the woman God

> Look inside yourself with open eyes and see who's really in there.

created. See her, embrace her, and honor her by insisting on your right to choose the life you are meant to live.

My hope is that you will see your life as I see mine, as a vast array of choices that can bring you closer to the person you long to be. My dream is for you to bring into your life whomever you cherish and whatever you desire by deciding, as I have, precisely who you are and what you need to be happy. Your life is waiting for you to claim it; it's all in the choosing. May you choose wisely and well.

ADDITIONAL NOTES

ADDITIONAL NOTES

ADDITIONAL NOTES

ADDITIONAL NOTES

Additional Notes

ADDITIONAL NOTES

ADDITIONAL NOTES

ADDITIONAL NOTES

ADDITIONAL NOTES

ADDITIONAL NOTES